Turn Down the Volume

By:
Dr. Solomon Tention

Copyright © Solomon Tention

All rights reserved.

No part of this book may be reproduced or used in any manner without the prior written permission of the copyright owner, except for the use of brief quotations in a book review.

Contents

Acknowledgments 1
Chapter 1 2
   Let's get this out the way..RIGHT NOW 2
Chapter 2 12
   What Are Insecurities? 12
Chapter 3 22
   You still have purpose 22
Chapter 4 31
   The Cure for Insecurities 31
Chapter 5 44
   F*****(Forget) People 44
Chapter 6 66
   Signs You Care Too Much About People! 66
Chapter 7 78
   I Just Want To Be Successful 78
Chapter 8 103
   Closing 103

Acknowledgments

I dedicate this project to you. I pray that you find tools, perspectives, and insights from my life's journey to inspire you to evolve into your highest self. It doesn't matter what you have been through at this point of your life. If you are reading this book at this moment, allow it to serve as the start of your new beginning. You are about to change the world!

Imperfectly on purpose . . .

Chapter 1
Let's get this out the way.. RIGHT NOW

Thank you for purchasing this book. Together we will turn down the volume of our insecurities, negative beliefs about success, and the people who perpetuate them. I am proud to say that I am a believer, an imperfect man of God, and God serves as the source of everything in my life. Therefore, I will always share my insights on how God has influenced my life. I understand that my readers come from different walks of life and have different faiths. Regardless of your beliefs, as you read this book I hope you can fill in the "blanks" and apply the principles to your life. I believe that this book's insights are applicable in every area of your life, no matter who you are or where you in your journey today.

Most of the time I feel like I have had more failures than successes in many areas of my life. However, I wrote this book because through a lot of self-work, I discovered that every failure in my life could be traced back to three key "pain points" that we will discuss in this book: *insecurities*, *people*, and *unhealthy beliefs* about *success*. These factors attempted to block me from experiencing the true success and purpose that God had in mind for my life. Everything I wanted was already there for me, I just couldn't access it fully yet. Despite many setbacks, I am grateful that God has brought me to a point where I can use my life's testimony to inspire others.

I am still evolving as a person and I am far from perfect! Each day I make mistakes and just like you find myself discovering new things about myself while doing the necessary self-work to evolve to my highest self. It's an interesting dynamic because with each success in my life, I can also point to an area that I am still working on. Ive just learned to not reflect as much on what I am working on and be greatful for where I am going. I also think that many of you can relate to my experience, which is why I decided to write this book.

There was a point in my life when I didn't celebrate key milestones because I was fixated on the work I needed to do to achieve the next goal. I was always on the next "thing" or project that I found to have value. I never took those small moments to reflect and celebrate the journey. I have since learned to accept the reality of life that we are all truly evolving each day. With each generation, there comes new growth, perspectives, and insights, which should be one of the great things about life that we embrace. We should take time every so often throughout our daily grind to reflect on how far we have come and to count our wins. Just this week while finishing up this book I was watching a sermon series on gratitude and the pastor discussed how we should take time each day to journal and reflect on every single thing that we should be grateful for. The series focused on teaching listeners on how even when things are looking, this act of humility will show us just how many milestones we can celebrate, both the big and small. I challenge you as now and has you read this book to reflect on your milestones.

I always mention on my podcast, blog, and other platforms where I present content that "I don't have all the answers, but I do believe I have perspective that will challenge you to perhaps make the decision to make some meaningful shifts in your own life. I believe this book will provide you with a unique perspective that will encourage you to think deeply about where you are today in your growth and the world around you. I am not implying that "my way" is "right" and your way is "wrong", as we are all "right" from our individual perspectives. Instead, view this book as a tool that prompts self-reflection. Engage in a series of self-evaluations to assess how you have been moving through life. What have been some of your roadblocks? do you always feel like you take one step forward and ten steps back? If so unpack that more to identify where the issues may be coming from.

The benefit of reading a book like this is that it provides you with the opportunity to gain perspective that is not biased centered by your friends or family members who might tell you what you want to hear. Even with the best intentions, our loved ones may not always tell you the full truth. So when you experience challenges, you might struggle to connect to opportunities for true accountability and growth due to the *intentional* or *intentional* faced of safety provided by these two groups. Don't operate in fear, it's actually a good thing to self-evaluate and check your beliefs and assumptions, the mere fact that you are able to do this type of inner work is not only healthy but also truly a blessing. We all have to live with some scars and residue from our past. However, if we are alive in this present moment to address and heal those scars, this is where the blessing resides. Awareness is the blessing! You getting to do the work is the blessing. There are many who are no longer with us, and I can almost guarantee that for some during their last days wished they had just one more chance to go back and redo some things, forgive that individual, or pursue that dream. Give yourself more grace and embrace this process. Give yourself the space to both evaluate and perhaps adopt new beliefs and healthy habits from those beliefs. Even if you were wrong…

This book does not follow a ten-step guide promising to solve all of your issues with insecurities, people, or beliefs about success. However, I believe that with the right perspective, it could be an excellent tool start to your inner work. My life's purpose is to create ecosystems that help millennials experience holistic success. One way I live that out in the entrepreneurship space is through a sense of commitment to inspiring millennials and men worldwide to live imperfectly on purpose.

Why? Because purpose saved my life, and I have discovered that by accessing your true self, living on purpose, and serving to make an impact is one of the most fulfilling things you can do with your time here on earth.

My journey has taught me that purpose is where you find true protection, provision, direction, and healing. Living a life on purpose means living a life of abundance in every aspect, not because you're perfect, but because you have chosen to live out God's will for your life. God is concerned with your "yes," and the work he has created you to do, not with you having everything together. Regardless of your mistakes he can still use you to achieve great things. This realization has inspired me to ensure that other millennials experience full, healthy, and productive lives while also being committed to their purpose and using their gifts and talents to impact the world around them.

Throughout the upcoming chapters, you'll notice that I frequently use the phrase "turn down the volume." This phrase is a metaphor that refers to anything, person, experience, or outside "voice" in our lives that prevents us from being connected to the true source from which we should seek direction from. I also want to challenge you now to take a few moments to reflect, get out a notebook, and ask yourself a series of questions. Have you turned up the volume of "people" higher than your goals, desires, and life's purpose? where have the opinions of "people" been louder than the true source in your life? what do you really think success is? what are those insecurities that you haven't addressed? and finally, do you "project" an image perfection. We will also spend a significant amount of time in this book discussing purpose. I believe that you can't help people *create* purpose, but only to discover the purpose that's already within them. There are three questions that I would like you to reflect on as you begin to consider who you are and what work you were created to do. Ask yourself: what's the need?, who are the people that might need you?, and what's the connection to your story? Once you have your answers, return to this chapter after finishing the book and ask yourself these same questions again. Take some notes and compare your responses. Afterwards make some healthy commitments and goals to move forward in the areas where you've found gaps and self-work is needed.

Chapter 2

What Are Insecurities?

The goal of this chapter is to inspire you to view insecurities from a different perspective. It will challenge your thoughts on insecurities, asking you to examine how you see them and define them, as well as the amount of power you may have given them throughout your life. We all experience some form of insecurity in our lives. Some insecurities develop due to the various traumas we've experienced, while others may have developed as a result of life's experiences, including the highs, lows, and everything in between. Regardless of how they've developed, insecurities are a natural element of our lives. We all have them, even the person who presents themselves as perfect in every from has an insecurity. That parent that was so hard on you with high expectations, that pastor that you listen to each week, the individuals that work at your favorite coffee shop, or that top level CEO that you see as a role model ... I have some news for you...they also have an insecurity. Over the last few years, I have seen a lot of content discussing how to "heal" from insecurities. However, I believe this approach may be somewhat flawed as it perpetuates the idea that we have to strive for some magical level of perfection.

There are some insecurities that we can completely heal from over time as we do the work, but there are also some insecurities that may remain with us for the rest of our lives. While they may not leave us, we can learn how to *manage* them by learning how to handle the triggers associated with them. From a spiritual context, God can use the insecurities we manage to help grow our faith and keep us humble. Consider this…. if you had it all together and was perfect with no worry, and could do everything perfectly while trying to live out this thing we call life, would you still need to depend on God? Perhaps you wouldn't pray for guidance, or maybe you would credit all of your success to yourself rather than acknowledging the God who helped you manage the not so good or fragile parts of yourself to achieve it. The Bible is full of examples of people whom God called to do great things, and they all had an insecurity or issue they were managing, for some of them, their first response was with an insecurity i.e. about how they weren't equipped, or what they didn't have. Many of them where even hesitant to accept and fulfill their specific purpose. However, in time the majority of them ultimately gave God their yes! What do you need to give God your yes for today?

Having some insecurities is not always necessarily a bad thing. By doing self-work and exercising your faith, you will find out which insecurities you can heal from and which ones you will need to manage throughout your life. Embracing this reality can be helpful because sometimes we try to be "perfect" without realizing that the perfection *we want* is not attainable. We actually are already perfect because we were *perfectly* made. I know, it may sound like a crazy concept, but it is worth considering.

Insecurities can be seen as tools or even catalysts in your story. They can serve as gifts that can help you sustain and remain humble as you progress in your purpose. For instance, when I started my podcast and had to be in front of the camera, I struggled with numerous insecurities. I said things to myself questions like, "how will people perceive me?", "what will they think of my overall message after listening to an episode?", and "I'm not creative and what if people don't like the presentation". I also didn't like how I spoke or sounded and I worried that people wouldn't appreciate my communication style. What's also interesting is that I never saw this issue come up in my professional world, but it was something about embarking on the entrepreneur journey that caused me to execute things at a different level. That different level exposed some things about me that I didn't necessarily like. Every time I thought about starting the podcast, I found myself confronted with these negative thoughts that served as a foundation for my insecurity. So what was at the root of my insecurity? I disliked being in the spotlight. I secretly preferred to work behind the scenes, not because it was where my skills best aligned, but because I spent the majority of my childhood feeling unloved, unseen, that I was a burden to people, and rejected. Because of these experiences, I created a pseudo "safe space" in my mind where I was present but "hiding in the back," as this made me feel secure… my insecurities served as my counselor.

We often fail to launch the things God has called us to do because we get trapped in unhealthy cycles of evaluation. Imagine if I had stayed stuck in my own evaluation, I would have never launched the Solomon Tention Podcast or written my first book series, The King Me. These projects have not only helped me grow personally, but have also increased my knowledge about the intersection of education and entrepreneurship, and served as a door to helping pave the way for so many opportunities to impact others that I could have never imagined. I have seen first hand how my podcast and books have impacted listeners and guests around the world. This would have never happened if I had not reframed my mindset, changed how I viewed insecurities, and followed God's plan for my life.

What's unique about God is that when we have the right type of relationship with him, we find that he has amazing things in store for us. His vision for our lives is much bigger than what we could ever imagine. He also loves us so much that he will wait until we are ready to be accountable, accept his hand, and be willing to do the self-work. He loves us so much that he will withhold the best things from our lives until we are ready, and can best serve the people that he has called us to help. He is patient and will meet us where we are to help change the trajectory of our lives. But we MUST take that first step. Don't allow insecurities to become the blocker to the life you desire.

When we adopt a mindset like the famous Nike slogan "just do it," we find that the concerns, evaluations, or negative self-talk that we have in our minds either don't matter anymore, or they visit us but don't stay long in our subconscious. With each step, God will send us a sign that we are moving in the right direction. Our confidence will begin to grow, and we will grow as individuals overall. Our brand will improve and our faith will grow because we are constantly asking God to help us grow with the insecurities we're managing. When we adopt this type of mindset, after some time with the consistency of us just putting one foot in front of the other, we'll look back and say to ourselves, "What was I so insecure about in the first place? I got this..."

So how did I get change my mindset? I stopped caring about how people viewed me! I shifted my focus to the assignment that God had for my life. I understood that it wasn't my job to do everything perfectly or worry about negative opinions from people. My job was to share the message and allow those individuals who align and receive the message to do so and those that don't... don't. Everything else is not my focus and is out of my control. Making this mindset shift has caused me to experience a level of comfort in entrepreneurship and other leadership spaces where I thought I had insecurities. Give God your insecurities ... and just do it!

Chapter 3

You still have purpose

I truly believe that doing purposeful work i.e. living your life's purpose, and fulfilling your true mission in life allows you to experience the best form of healing. Perhaps you have been reflecting on your life and have realized that your insecurities have been louder than your true inner compass. You may realize that you allowed your insecurities to talk you out of some dope experiences you wanted to have. Regardless, I want to remind you that just because you have insecurities, it doesn't mean that you don't have a purpose. In fact, your insecurities can serve as the foundation that God uses to help you impact and change the lives of generations assigned to you. If you have purchased this book, it is because you have a desire to grow and evolve into your highest self.

You may have also recognized that you have untapped talents, gifts, and contributions that you want to share with the world. You are tired of going and circles and ready for your next.

In our minds there may always be two worlds. The "first world" is filled with ideas, interests, and plans to make a positive impact in today's society. But then there is the "second world", where a small voice likes to have a mental "date night" with your insecurities. Negative experiences in our lives serve one purpose, to make the voices in the second world louder than the first. That voice may remind you of your insecurities, past mistakes, or traumas in your life. It may say things like, "I know you want to do ____, but remember that you are not ____," or "Remember when you had ____

experience and ____ happened?" "You are not _____ enough to do____."

Remember that these negative voices don't define you and they don't determine your purpose. Instead, let your insecurities be the fuel that ignites your passion and drives you towards purpose. Use these voices as a reminder of your strength and resilience. Think about it this way; those voices wouldn't come if they didn't know you had the power to "birth" something. Use these negative voices to empower you to make a positive impact in the world.

Insecurities "unchecked" can rule your life. They have such a hold us on mentally that we also haven't talked about it, nor even seek out spaces to deal with them. As a result of this unchecked part of ourselves, our potential becomes stagnated. I truly believe that if an idea exists in your mind it's because you were meant to bring that idea to life. That idea was meant for you and only you to lead. There are people that who would benefit from your idea but will never experience the gifts from your talents because you won't launch it.

Throughout the growth of my own relationship with Christ, my view and perspective on purpose have taken a major shift. I believe that when we are born, God "pre-loaded" a message into us, which is some work that we were meant to do to impact the community around us. He also gave us the necessary gifts, talents, and traits, all designed to help us fulfill that mission. However, it is also important to understand that while we already have a purpose, the way in which we serve to live it out will always look different.

Your relationship with Christ will help you discover *the way* in which he desires you to fulfill your purpose. For example, if your purpose is to advocate for youth in a certain space, that might look different depending on the "function", such as being a judge within the juvenile justice system, starting your own non-profit, or public speaking. Regardless of which function you serve; your purpose is still being fulfilled as an advocate for youth. Within the Kingdom, God sees all of our purposes the same and celebrates when we make those contributions, no matter how big or small. This is why I stand on the principle that no one is greater than the next. We are all sinners saved by grace and here on earth having a human experience, attempting to live out the work that God has placed in our lives. We all know that every choice we make in life comes with consequences, but we rarely discuss the impact of not living a purposeful life.

What does life look like when we fail to fulfill God's calling or be the person he intended us to be? I believe that there are subtle consequences to not following our purpose, and when insecurities often drive our decisions. One of the consequences of not launching the work that God created us to do is that we deprive a generation of people assigned to us and our gift. Those individuals also never get the opportunity to experience the growth and inspiration they need for their life's journey. You may think that if you don't do it, someone else with the same talent can, but that is not congruent with God's original design. God created each of us with a specific purpose and assignment for a particular group of people. We are unique, and there is no one else who can connect with them like we can. These people were set aside for us, and only our unique and specific contributions can impact their lives. We are a 1:1 with our purpose, no one else can fulfill that role like the one originally designed to lead it. There is only one you!

We must commit to doing the work to ensure that our insecurities do not drown out our gifts, identity, or control every aspect of our lives. We need to ensure that our insecurities do not over shadow what we believe our purpose is. At one point in my life, I thought my purpose was to become a Family Attorney, and when that did not work out like I planned, I attempted to become a I.O Psychologist. Both were great areas to serve and make an impact, looked good on paper with the plan I developed. However, those were places of influences that I chose and were not aligned with who God created me to be, and the space/function he desired me to fulfill. To be completely honest those choices were rooted in my insecurities, specifically of the "little me", "big you" insecurity that I discussed in earlier chapters. This mindset led me down the wrong path and to make some poor decisions that affected every area of my life. My insecurities blocked my view of self and the voice of who God was consistently communicating who he intended me to be. I wanted to make an impact, but only on my terms in the way that I was comfortable for me. God always had different plans. His plan involved me stepping out of my comfort zone the shadows and fulfilling my purpose in a big way. His planned required me to be "stretched" and uncomfortable in every area of my life. Behind the stretching and feelings of discomfort, he has been with me every step of the way, even when I made mistakes. Don't allow your insecurities to cause you to miss out on the blessings behind being "stretched". No matter how you see yourself or your insecurities now, you still have purpose....

Chapter 4

The Cure for Insecurities

Just do it! I believe that's the cure for insecurities. I don't have a magical quote, exercise, or anything that you might have expected to help you navigate this. JUST DO IT! You must understand that with some insecurities, it's hard for us to move forward because negative experiences in our lives create memories, and those memories result in lies we tell ourselves. We will talk about "believing lies" more as we go through this chapter but first, I want to share with you an example of what it looks like to "believe a lie".

For example, let's say you are thirty years old and when you reflect on the origin of your first insecurity, you've felt as though you've always had issues engaging in groups of any size, or networking.

Each time you are faced with these types of situations in any capacity, you found it difficult to make new friends, and become almost borderline socially awkward. For years, you have identified this feeling as an insecurity, but as you do your inner work to identify the source, you find the negative emotions around meeting and engaging with new people actually started when you were ten years old and rejected from the friend group during recess. No one wanted to play with you, and you found yourself alone in the playground and was unable to find a new group of friends that you felt comfortable with, so you played alone each day.

Within this example you might be able to see how at the age of ten something in your brain, along with the fact that you more than likely lived in a home environment where your interpersonal development was not a priority, impacted you in such a way as a child that made you believe negative perceptions about yourself. You believed that there was something wrong with you, i.e. "the lie", and now your thirty, having grown up almost half of your life being insecure about engaging with people due to an un-addressed rejection experience that occurred when you were ten. This perceived insecurity may or may not have prevented you from experienced so many opportunities within your life.

In this example, we see just how easily we can "believe the lie" of negative things that have transpired in our childhood trauma or underdevelopment. These lies then subsequently birth characteristics, personality traits, and insecurities that were NEVER supposed to be a part of our identity. Take some time at this point of your reading to think about what areas in your life have you "believed the lie" and how has it impacted not only how you live your life but also how you see yourself. You must combat the lie with what God says about you, different types of affirmations, and be committed to do the needed inner work of evolving to your highest self. Stop believing the lies!

I have found that once we start taking the necessary steps towards our purpose, true healing awaits us on that journey. Purpose is the ultimate healer of our insecurities. This healing energy is unique because as we heal towards our purpose, we simultaneously evolve into the person that God intended us to be, not the person that negative experiences or others have forced us to become. God honors our commitment and meets us where we are. He provides us with the grace and peace to fulfill our purpose and helps us grow in the process. We must trust in the one who created us to guide us in the right direction despite our insecurities; rather than relying on people or even ourselves at times.

The first key strategy to help you turn down the volume of your insecurities is to first learn how to be okay with yourself. Learn how to accept love and appreciate who you are and the person God created you to be. Learning to be "ok with you" is one of the keys to being content and happy with where you are presently. This doesn't mean that you now have an excuse to not work on yourself, not grow, or even try to address some of the things that you need to work on because we are all flawed. We will all be doing self-work until our last day. The moment we stop discovering and working to improve things about ourselves is probably the moment we leave this earth. However, for the things about you that are a part of God's original design, you have to learn to be okay with them. You must embrace and stand on the principles and values that come along with you, otherwise no one else will.

How do you know what elements of your characteristics, gifts, and traits were a part of your original design? Think back to the earliest and happiest part of your childhood; before the trauma, hurt, rejection, etc. The "you" that you find there, or i.e. the inner child that is looking back at you, characteristics and all, is the "you" that God originally created you to be. At that time in your life, you were innocently displaying all of the characteristics that God needed you to have to live out your life's purpose. You have to go back to that place to heal!

There was a point in my life where I found myself feeding into people's opinions about me. Those opinions then developed an insecurity within me that I carried throughout my personal and professional life. I faced the difficult challenge of attempting to live out my purpose while also developing into the young man that God had called me to be. Due to my own insecurities, my mind was conditioned to live in "survival mode", so much so that during my doctoral commencement ceremony, what was supposed to be a celebration of the highest academic degree a person can earn in my field, I never even took that time to take it all in. I just saw it as another milestone and while on stage, I spent more time thinking about a group of students that I had planned to take to Austin, TX the next week as soon as I returned to the office than this great achievement. I didn't take the chance to reflect on the journey and celebrate the gravity of the moment. The trauma behind our insecurities can rob us of every good moment.

There were also so many times when people would give me their idea of what a successful black scholar should look like. Everyone had their own vision of how I should "be" except for me. So, I subconsciously decided to "dumb down" parts of myself. I dumbed down myself because I wanted to be "accepted", and hoped people would forget about me and limit their opinions. I worked so hard to seem less threatening to peers. However, as the years went on I learned that some of those very things about me that I "turned down" were the key aspects of my personality and attributes that I later found out were exactly what God needed for me to connect to a new generation of future leaders and scholars. I turned down parts of my true-self because I wanted to fit the stereotype or check the preferable box of what an educated black man was supposed to look like and what he was supposed to do. I've worked in environments where people would "code switch" and reduce parts of themselves for the sake of keeping their job, and to a certain extent, it seemed normal. It seemed like the "deal" you had to make if you wanted to be black and successful.

When I was an up and coming leader, I bore a heavy responsibility and often felt the energy of people feeling "threatened" by me inside my own professional and even some personal groups. It was a difficult time because I discovered that people didn't seem to embrace the "professional i.e. Dr. Tention" or "personal, i.e. Solomon" me. I lived in a constant state of confusion and found myself fluctuating between two identities to make people happy, my insecurity about people became louder than my true self. Learning to accept myself was a big step towards growth in this area. I learned that God created me to be a "hybrid" with the unique ability to communicate with people from all walks of life and in different sectors, and all parts of me were unique and of value. That tension that I was living in trying to balance both worlds was never supposed to exist! God had a specific plan that allowed me as a millennial a "seat at the table" but still connected to the issues, relatable, and able to connect/adapt to any environment. This was all a part of his plan and had to learn what my comfort level was and be willing to show up as my "full-self", no matter what space I occupied.

Once I became okay with self, I saw the value I brought to the table as the unapologetically me.... Solomon Tention. God created me on PURPOSE and wanted to use everything about me to make an impact through my purpose. I made a commitment never to let someone's opinion cause me to go against myself, but I first had to know self in purpose.

The second strategy is to "stop believing the lie." We discussed earlier how negative experiences in our lives create memories, and we often believe things about ourselves that are not true. We must stop believing the lie and come up with a new story about ourselves and the environment around us. The entity telling this lie is our inner critic, we all have one and he/she lives with us. They wake up with us and, with our permission, are always willing and able to counsel and drive our lives in their desired direction.

Our inner voice critiques us, tells us what we don't want or shouldn't do, or why something is not going to be great. Insecurities are based on lies, coupled with the inner critic who communicates those lies constantly. As mentioned above one of the strategies to stop believing the lies is through daily affirmations. Affirmations can be in the form of scripture references, or phrase like statements are healthy tools that give you the opportunity to combat the lie with positive, re-enforcement self-talk. Affirmations serve as "facts" or desired attributes about yourself and not the basis of a negative experience. Make a commitment today to no longer allow insecurities to control your life. Instead, accept yourself for who you are and who you are becoming, embracing everything that God has called you to be. You are not defined by your insecurities; they are simply a part of life. How you handle them will ultimately determine the type of life on purpose you will have. Take some time to reflect on what are some areas where you are insecure and repeat this affirmation, "today I will no longer give my insecurities power over my life, and will stop believing the lies".

Chapter 5
F*****(Forget) People

One of the first steps to reducing the impact of people and their opinions is to understand your audience. This concept may be new to you, but it's important to recognize that you have a specific audience, and it's not everyone. As we discussed in previous chapters, you were born with a purpose and a message to share with the world. There is a pre-determined group of people that you were created to reach with that message. Therefore, not everyone will like, love, support, align with, believe like, or support you.

Once you understand the specific focus of your purpose, and commit to evolving into your highest self, I believe you will know your audience. When you understand your audience, you can better discern who is for you and who is not. If people don't accept or reject you and your gifts, it's not a reflection of your worth or always a signal that you need to change. Instead it just simply means that they are not part of your intended audience, and it's really a natural aspect of life.

This principle can apply to any relationship in your life, whether personal or professional. When you are true to yourself and living out your God-given purpose, rejection from others doesn't make them "bad" people, they are just misaligned. Throughout this book, you may have noticed consistent themes connecting back to the importance of living a life on purpose, which is 100% intentional. Your ability to live a purposeful life is crucial because it enables you to avoid becoming subject to people's opinions and paradigms.

Neglecting to do this inner work can cause people to affect you negatively emotionally and in other harmful ways. For example, if someone says something negative about you, and you give it too much power, it can cause hurt more than it should. You find yourself spending so much time on that one person's negative perception about you that you forget to be "productive". You forget about your goals because you are so focused on why that may have had that opinion about you, or you chase their acceptance.

If you want to navigate "people" better, gain clarity on your audience. Who are the people that God created you to serve? Who are the people that best align with your values? Where should you go to find these people? Sometimes, we get hurt by people because we either placed them in the wrong position within our lives, or we are trying to serve an audience that we weren't built for. Again, this doesn't make them bad people, nor you a bad person, it just means that you're in the wrong location.

When we surround ourselves with the wrong audience and people in our lives, we expose ourselves to a lifetime of pain and long term psychological setbacks. I once heard on a podcast that "self-abuse is the greatest form of abuse". Allowing negative opinions and perceptions of others to affect us and to trigger a cycle of self-evaluation that is unnecessary causes us to go down a tunnel of confusion, i.e. self-abuse. We must embrace who we are and be our authentic selves, even if it feels uncomfortable and unfamiliar. I have found joy, peace, and success by being the person God created me to be, rather than the person others wanted me to be. Focus on surrounding yourself with those who support, hold accountable, and uplift you towards purpose.

Everybody has an opinion (especially on social media), and that's great, but remember that people's opinions of you have nothing to do with you. Their opinions of you are merely a projection of their own lived experience and perspective. People's opinions of you are based on the world that they currently live in, and sometimes exposes some of the negative things in them. Sometimes people can't deal with that emotionally properly and comes out as hurt thrown back at you. How much more productive we could be in the world if we all would just accept that we are all "right". Everyone is living in their reality, and therefore, to a certain extent, their perspective or opinion is "right"... right in their reality. Once a person has made up their mind about you or a situation, there is no need to convince them otherwise. I am writing this book from MY perspective, from the perspective of a millennial who has experienced enough highs and lows to write ten more books, from the perspective of someone who has been on the receiving end of God's grace and have made plenty of mistakes, and from the perspective of someone committed to inspire other millennials around the world to live life on purpose... It's just a perspective, not the rule. We work so hard to change people's perception of us without understanding that you can be in a room of ten other individuals, and each of those individuals will have a different perception of you. If you actually spent the time focusing on figuring out how to be ten different people to ten different people, think about how much self-harm you do to yourself when you live life this way. If trauma can get you to be overly concerned about people, you will never evolve to your highest self, i.e. the real you because there was so much time and effort given to appease others. Or you become a version of self-that's really a combined version of others. You wake up each day and put on a mask and go home empty and unfulfilled.

If you're engaging with a person who has a broken consciousness, they're going to see things from the perspective of someone that's broken... That's their reality, and it doesn't make them bad; that's just their perspective. For example, if you encounter a person who is entrepreneurial in nature, more than likely, they're going to see things and give their opinions of people and the world around them from the perspective of an entrepreneur. People's opinions have nothing to do with you and everything to do with them! People's negative opinions of you are not an indictment of you and who you are. Even if you had a bad day, one person's experience of you is not a "period" of your story, it's a "comma" .... give yourself grace.

All people have opinions but you get to choose what you accept. I am not saying to become an egotistical person who no one can provide you with a healthy perspective or mentorship, but what I am saying is there are some healthy methods that you could use in learning how to "vet" opinions. You should vet opinions to determine if they are opinions you should "accept" or "reject". Everything in your life will really start to evolve when you know who you are and your purpose. Your purpose gives you a sense of confidence, focus, and can serve as an internal navigation system/advisor. When you have done the work and are centered on your core, you should then only accept an opinion if it is meant to help you better evolve into your purpose; and even then, it should not be your first time hearing it. No one should ever be in a position to tell you something about yourself first that completely surprises you. "People" should never be your "single" source of truth; if any their thoughts about how you show up should be a mere confirmation of what God has shown you in your personal time with him and as a result of the inner work that you have already done. God would never send someone in your life who does not help you evolve into the person he initially created you to be. He only sends you relationships that are needed to help you fulfill your mission in the kingdom. We must learn to see things from God's perspective and not on our own understanding. But again the key here is that you must be in purpose to make these mindset changes.

Understanding when "I should" or "should not" consider someone's opinion was one of the key areas I had to grow spiritually in. When I was younger, if someone gave me a critique I would go into this cycle of evaluation because I figured, who better to give me insight on how I show up in the world than the people I interact with every day. I would take that information and go to God or mentors and say, "Please help me with ___ and ___, etc., etc." This person noticed___ so maybe it's something I should work on. Finally, one-day God challenged me in our relationship because I would go to him with the opinions of "people" and never placing him as the source. He challenged me to understand that he was not my personal "consultant", or someone that helped me do what I wanted to do, or that I should only spent time with him when I had a problem to solve. During those hard growth moments God showed me that he DID NOT NEED people to correct me. But if he CHOOSES to use them, it will either be as a confirmation of what he has already told me, opportunities for relationships that help me better evolve into the man he created me to be, or he may use interactions with people to serve as a warning sign. But regardless, I should seek him as the true source. He is the leader not me. Use my story and some of the strategies that we have discussed so far to reflect and to build internal systems to "vet" the people around you. When you engage in this work you might be surprised of the type of relationships that you will need to remove.

You should also accept that not everyone will like you. When you know how God sees you, who you are, and your purpose, and stand on specific values about yourself, you will not only learn that people will not always like you, but to some degree, expect it. This doesn't mean that you think you are "better" than others or that the next person doesn't have value. It just means that you may not align with everyone, and that's okay. For example, I am not only passionate about all millennials living a life of purpose but also specifically focused on helping to ensure that men around the world live a full life of purpose, leading within their families, communities, and so on. I understand that biblically men serve as the foundation of all things in the earth and that we must do the work to take back our place and function in our natural order. Therefore, if you are someone who does not value the role of men as leaders in society, or can be influencers in the earth, I expect you not to like me because what I represent and my value system is counter to your views, and again this separation also doesn't make you a bad person.

If I continued to factor people into my decision-making, how I built goals for my life, or how I saw myself, I would have never become the man I am today. Your goal and assignment in life, is to stay close to whatever higher being you believe in and seek that higher being for your identity, guidance, counsel, and decision-making…not people. Embracing seasons of alone time so that you can learn to love yourself, grow, develop, and evolve into your highest self can serve a vital role in mastering how to not be impacted by people. This work also builds a strong sense of really about self-awareness.

I conducted some research on brain studies that have taken place over the last couple of years and it was interesting to see how researchers examined the brain. According to the Smithsonian National Museum of Natural History, joining a tribe and being accepted by others was critical to survival. Even though we do not need tribes to survive in today's world, we still biologically have the desire other people for companionship and stimulation. Humans are social animals, and we were also biblically built for community. By nature, we have this inert need to be accepted by others. When you examine your ancestral roots you find that being a part of tribes and community was critical to survival. Our un-healed trauma can turn our nature against us causing us live our life for the acceptance of people. Brain images indicate that both positive and negative feedback from others causes a chemical response in our brains. A fear of negative evaluation is particularly strong when it comes from a trusted source; especially for people with social anxiety, low self-esteem, and those who grew up without emotional support. People who lack the necessary emotional support are more likely to care too much about what others think of them. Taking some time to understand your background is essential and you must always give ourselves grace. Sometimes along the way, life happens and we lose our sense of self. Regardless of the hurt caused from negative experiences, you still have an assignment. You have a purpose, value, and you are needed on this earth. When you were born, at the same time you were pre-destined to serve a certain group of people who were going to love you, accept you, and need you to be great. Your voice is needed to make an impact! Another way to think about this is that when you confidently know who you are, your purpose, what God has created you to do, and you have this belief that you are here to make an impact ….why would you give the power of who you are, what you're meant to be, what you do, and how you see yourself to another person? If God loves and approves of your work, it doesn't really matter about what anyone else thinks.

Trauma can confuse and challenge our identity about who we are. As a result of that confusion, we find ourselves being enamored with people and false "movies" that are on repeat in our heads. If this is you, you always seem have to be around people, travel with people, talk to people each day, have people by our house, seek people for opinions and ideas. We find ourselves loving this idea of people because secretly we don't like the person we see in the mirror looking back at us. We have so many different types people around us that it blocks us from spending much needed alone time. We can't hear because we have all these voices in our ear giving us directions and advice about every area of our life. We need time to learn, grow, self-correct, heal, and evolve to our highest self. Of course I know that some of you may be extroverts but I want to challenge you to do some honest reflection here to determine if your attachment to people is at a comfortable and healthy level for your growth.

There are some times in your life where I believe you have to walk alone, no matter how scary it might be. We fail to establish boundaries with people, and we keep toxic relationships with friends and family members because we don't want to upset them. We don't evolve and grow into our highest selves because we are too worried about pleasing others. We may have interests in other areas, but we're consumed by our concern for people. We ask ourselves questions like, what if they don't agree? what if I'm by myself? what if I loss people? how will people view me? etc. etc. the cycle evaluation can get so deep that you "think" yourself into anxiety and an overall unhealthy mindset.

Another strategy to help you not feel so rejected from negative views from people that hinder your growth... go find your community. When I began to surround myself with like-minded people, i.e., creators, entrepreneurs, podcasters, etc., there is never hate or jealousy, only the energy towards everyone in the community being in the spirit of correction, accountability, and becoming better in my craft. I wonder how our lives would shift if we learned how to get around the RIGHT people. I want you to be okay with negative opinions about you because they are only designed to keep you from progressing to where God is taking you. I've learned recently that it's not even kingdom to care about or look for other people to like you. *See Jesus teaching his disciples in Matthew 5:10*

Sometimes I wonder how God our father must feel when we decide to be someone else that he didn't create us to be. I would imagine that to him he would be hurt that we don't like what he created. Just as our earthly fathers would feel hurt if his children rejected parts of him in them. In my own conviction

I had to realize that the best version of Solomon was connected to the authentic me fully connected to a sense of self and purpose. God loves us so much and he spent his precious time creating us, giving us a specific purpose, and even equipping us with unique talents, traits, personality characteristics, etc. that were all necessary for us to be uniquely successful within our purpose. Only for us to allow "people" to cause us to become something we were never created to be.

We also can't take people's positive opinions about us too seriously as well. I know when you picked up this book you probably thought that this chapter was just going to be about people's *negative* opinions, but I like to keep you thinking with different perspectives. Your focus should essentially and solely be on your purpose. How can an overly embracing of positive opinions of me impact my focus? Wouldn't that motivate me, encourage me, inspire me to do more? I've learned to take positive opinions for just what they were, someone making a positive comment about how I showed up in a certain space. You show appreciation and gratitude, and you may take a moment to really reflect and be grateful for whatever growth or achievement that you might have. But your focus should shift back to your purpose; you can't stay there. Get back to being purpose-minded, stay humble and focused. This mental fitness is important because while we are in this big experiment called life, positive compliments are great, but an over-engagement of these types of opinions might develop within us sense of pride and arrogance that ultimately becomes our pitfall. God will in turn not allow us to access everything he has for us because we can't be trusted. We can't get "too high" nor "too low". We must master the art of just enjoying the "middle", unshakeable, focused, connected… on purpose. Sometimes when you receive a lot of positive opinions, you might start to feel invincible and believe that nothing can go wrong. You may even start to think that you cannot make mistakes or lose everything, simply because everyone is praising you… so you must be "great". If you want to sustain purpose and live under an open heaven, you must maintain this level of humility.

Chapter 6

Signs You Care Too Much About People!

I want to start this chapter with a disclaimer that my list is based on personal experience. It is not from any clinical research, or any other mental health related publication. However, here are some signs from my own life experience that you might care too much about people.

The first sign is that you change yourself in response to criticism, regardless of what it is and who it comes from. We talked somewhat about this in the previous chapter, but everybody that critiques you "impacts" you. You have no "funneling" or "evaluation" system to determine where the critique comes from. You have no level of discernment. Anybody who criticizes you makes you believe it as time to make changes in your life. For example, if there are ten people in a room, if I tried to become the version of me that people had in their heads, I would probably lose my mind and be too exhausted to become my true self because I am so busy being who everyone else perceives me to be. I am also too tired for purpose. I can't hear God's critiques and counsel about me because I am so concerned with people. When you live your life this way, you will die as a person "liked by people" but who did not fulfill their mission. You ultimately became a slave to people. What are you going to do with the time you have in life? If you can breathe, that means you have life, and if you have life, that means there is something that you are here to do.

The second sign you care too much about people is that you let other people "make decisions for you". There is no clarity, purpose, and or self-directed vision. You must get to a space in your life where you are able to make decisions that are comfortable for you and your journey. You can't run anyone's race. It's harmful to you as an individual and thus essentially counterproductive. On one of my social media platforms, I posted the quote", I don't care if you have to do it alone, if you got to do it broke, if you have to do it one step at a time, or if you have to do it slow, it doesn't matter. Everything that God has put on your heart to do, run your race, even if no one agrees. Only you know what God has shown you about your life. Life has taught me that as you begin to "do", God will send people your way who are also doing, they will become your tribe, "gap fillers", support system, mentors, sponsors, etc. They will serve as the catalyst in your life that God uses to shift you in a new direction. Opportunities in your purpose are limitless, who knows you find yourself in front of the crowds that you were meant to serve and they were meant to hear your story.

When I first started building my podcast, I found the content inspiring, but I was also concerned about who would connect with the focus. I would always ask myself, "how will I find guests"? These were all things that in the grand scheme of starting any business, didn't really matter, but at the time I saw so many others on their entrepreneurship path and found myself comparing. So, I decided to just start "doing" and create a strategy that worked for me. I began recording interviews, posting content, and promoting my show with any budget I could come up with. After a few months, I started to connect with the people who were meant to hear my message all along. I received countless messages about how my podcast was helping people grow, and my followers started to share my content. Some of my content also started to trend and go viral (at least viral to my standards). As time went on, I no longer had to join countless groups to find guests (although that is still a good method,). We are now blessed to have a waiting list of guests who want to appear on the show. We are now on your first nationwide tour and there have already been so many connections made amongst the guest that they will use to further their journey. These great things wouldn't have happened if I didn't take that leap of faith, and follow my own path. There is someone else's blessing tied to your obedience and self-directedness. God needs to know that you can be self-directed with directions given to fulfill his work in your life. He will bless your efforts if you turn down the volume of that voice in your head that's worried about what others think and just start doing! There are people in your niche who are waiting for you, just be authentic and they will come. A great person to study biblically to help you improve in this area is Jesus' earthly dad, Joseph or essentially any influential leaders throughout history from M.L King to Walt Disney, or Bill Gates, and many others. They all had to at some vital point make some key decisions for self, understanding that others may not agree with them.

The third sign that you care too much about people is when you struggle to set and maintain boundaries. You may believe that setting expectations for people in your life will cause them to disrespect you or even leave you. As a result, you limit yourself to a small group of people and adjust your behavior based on their expectations. This pattern of behavior can become a norm and is often driven by subconscious beliefs about yourself and others. It's essential to examine why you struggle with setting boundaries and work towards changing this pattern. Those who respect you will honor your boundaries, and those who don't are showing you who they truly are. Their unwillingness to adjust shows you how much they value the relationship. These principles can apply to just about in every area of your life, the workplace, church, the gas station, it doesn't matter. Set boundaries for yourself!

Not maintaining boundaries is a sign that you have turned up the volume of "people". We often fail to establish healthy boundaries because of our own traumas. Once you engage in this work, if you find yourself with zero friends, that's okay because at least you know that you eliminated friends from your life who disrespected you by disregarding your boundaries. After this boundary and relationship realignment work, focus on healing, growth, and evolving to embrace new forms of relationships that align with your boundaries. Sometimes, we fear developing relationships because we feel like there is no one else in the world who will respect who we truly are, so we conform to the people around us. We then decide to be someone else, and that someone often has no boundaries. We are liked by everyone but respected by none. You especially need boundaries with people and even for yourself if you are going to commit to living a life on purpose. Your boundaries and standards should never change just because someone else disagrees with them.

The next sign that you care too much about people, and the one I struggled with at different points in my life, is being a "perfectionist". In my early twenties, I was young in my career and focused on making my mark in education. I was trying to build a portfolio that would open up doors for me in the future. I also knew the pressure I would be under as a young black administrator, with all eyes on me. I knew my margin for error was small in comparison to other colleagues, so I worked hard to manage people's opinions about me. I led with the pressure in my subconscious of not wanting to promote the narrative that young and black administrators can't ascend to leadership roles, or can't handle the work. I wanted to leave a legacy that would promote a culture where young black leaders who come after me would have the same or more opportunities. Thus essentially my concern for people in this environment convinced me that I had to be "perfect".

I didn't realize at the time that my commitment to purpose and doing what God asked me to do in the seat was all I really needed to do, nothing more, nothing less. I had to learn that I couldn't control people's perspectives. I'm not saying don't carry yourself as a professional, but you're not going to be perfect. I often tell my staff now, and when I hired them to not expect me to be perfect. I always remind them that I'm human and won't be able to meet those expectations; even if I tried. However, I do communicate to others that I may work with professionally or even in my business that i'm committed to the idea that when I make a mistake, I will own it, apologize, and get it right.

When you care too much about people and constantly apologize this type of behavior causes you unknowingly open yourself up to manipulation.

Manipulators can notice that you're a "serial apologizer" and they use this to their advantage. They'll create confusing scenarios and communicate half-truths, knowing that you'll apologize even when you're not at fault. This is a manipulation tool they use to control you and distract you from the harm they're causing. Apologizing is fine, but make sure you're not a puppet in someone else's game. Only apologize when you've actually done something wrong.

The final sign that you might care too much about people is that you rarely say "no". You say yes to everything, even at your own expense, whether or not you have the capacity or resources. You enjoy saying yes and thrive on the rarity of saying no. I have found that it's important to embrace the power of saying no. Take some time each day to find some things or situations that you can say no to. It doesn't have to be big things but the goal is to get yourself in the habit of saying no. You will find that you have more strength to establish this boundary more than you think. Also remember that believe or not, people will be ok if you say no. If you want to know how someone truly feels about you, try telling them no. Exercise your option of saying no from time to time and observe their response. People will always show who they are, it's just about whether or not your eyes are open.

Chapter 7

I Just Want to Be Successful

The goal of this chapter is to prompt deeper reflection into your own life to determine what success really means to you. Contrary to popular belief it's possible to be successful in the wrong thing. At some point in our lives, we may have tried, or attempts have been made to convince us that success should equate to power, education, status, prestige, etc. While those things might be a byproduct of success, and in some ways enjoyable, I've learned that it's better to ensure your life's success is driven by a God-given purpose.

We all have been blessed with free will, and you can always do your own thing. However, the success that comes with purpose can provide you with another level of provision, safety, security, and direction. Not because you are perfect, but because of the idea that your success has everything to do with you submitting to God's will for your life. You are making the decision to be who God created you to be and not the person that others or your circumstances want you to be. In the Kingdom you look like our original father. Our success has nothing to do with us and our will. Instead, it has everything to do with being the person that God created us to be.

In my life I have come to understand that God measures success much differently than we do. On one of my podcast episodes I talked about the fact that many of us believe that our success is tied to a "title." However, it's really about the "function" by which we serve as a result of that title. For example, let's say you have been blessed to serve as a vice president of a major organization. It's not that God created you to be a vice president; it's deeper than what's on the surface. You were created to be a leader, and the specific assignment in your life calls for you to serve as vice president to make the desired impact. You are serving in that function because there's something in you that God wants to replicate throughout a large ecosystem ultimately to give him glory. God saw fit to give you access to a certain level of education required and access to a position to bring about his will and his message. Adopting this perspective, even someone who's a gifted plumber and volunteers part-time with youth because of a passion for changing the next generation can be "on purpose". From the "kingdom's perspective," that plumber is just as "successful" as this vice president. These are two individuals, who are using their gifts and talents to serve their purpose, while in different ways, God is pleased with both of their contributions to the earth. We sometimes place all of this emphasis on titles, education, etc., and that mindset places us in cycles of comparison and feelings of low self-worth. Sometimes we forget that Jesus was a carpenter... For example, my purpose is to build ecosystems to help millennials and men thrive and experience success. The function by which I serve in that purpose is as a college administrator, professor, and entrepreneur. I have been given the assignment of making impact in three distinct but connected areas. I have also been blessed with the background story, education, tools, etc., to "live out" that purpose in each space. But that's MY purpose and walk; your purpose and success will look different because it's unique to you and your story. Take some time here to reflect, make some connections and seek God for clarity on who you are.

When you succeed in God's way, opportunities will naturally come to you because you have made the decision to accept and walk in his will for your life. Once you commit to being on your purpose and submitting to the ultimate mission for your life, he will meet you where you are and as you grow, provide you access to opportunities already predestined for you. God also desires for you to fulfill his is will for your life because it's NOT ABOUT YOU. Even when you don't feel like you're making the right amount of money, I guarantee that if you align your life with your purpose and be the person God has created you to be, you will find that all of your needs and some of your wants will be met. I have never met someone who has struggled in any area of their lives from a resource standpoint after choosing a purposeful life. Do you really think God will not take care of your needs after you commit your life to him to do the work he put you here for? He is concerned with our message. We are all put here as unique problem solvers. God has given you gifts, talents, and characteristics needed to fulfill your purpose. If you choose to operate in your gift, you are guaranteed to be successful because your gifts are making contributions to the world. Your purpose is God's ultimate provision and what God sees as "success".

Consistent inner work is required if we want to be able to "handle" success. Sometimes, I think we are not as successful as we would like, not because we lack talent, skills, or competency, but because we may not be ready to handle success. God wants to protect us, and those that we are called to serve and thus he may withhold success from us until we are prepared for it. So, perhaps our frustration is unwarranted. Let do the work to be ready for success when it comes.

Here's a daily prayer that may be helpful:

Dear God, I am not yet where I want to be, but I won't get discouraged. I know it's because there's something in me that you are working on before you give it to me.

Please help me to do the hard inner work necessary to prepare me for success. Help me to be patient and trust in your plan for my life. Give me the strength and courage to face my fears and overcome any obstacles in my way. Help me to stay focused on my purpose and remain true to my values. Thank you for your constant love and guidance. Amen

Sometimes, we never reach the success that's for us because we lack wisdom. There's no golden ticket that can give someone more wisdom than you. Wisdom is the ability to acquire and apply existing knowledge. I've learned that when you show God that you have the ability to pursue wisdom, rather than perfection, he knows he can trust you any level of success. He knows that through every season, you will seek him to acquire and apply wisdom. He knows that no matter what level he gives you access to; you will still seek him as the source for direction. Pursuing wisdom also shows that you have the ability to shift. Reflect here about whether or not you can truly be trusted with success? What are some aspects of success that you are unsure about?

I think back to a recent experience where I assumed a new role in my full-time life. I was serving as the senior leader of a college, working to secure various levels of public and private funding that would ultimately impact staffing and services for black and brown college students. I remember praying to God, grateful for the new role but at the same time worried. My prayer was that this big role requires a lot of weight and responsibility. I knew the work was tied to my purpose, and I no doubt believed that I had the skill set to get the job done, but it didn't change the weight of a role like this. A few weeks into the role I found there was little margin for errors and each project was tied to real people getting the help they needed to experience success in their lives. My mistakes could result in not only a lack of funding to serve students but also the employees that whose salaries depended on re-occurring funding. During my prayer, God spoke to me like only a father could speak to a son and told me that he allowed me obtain this role to serve my purpose for your life, and that I was in the "seat" because he knew that I could handle it. He also had me look back at my portfolio and he reminded me that he had been preparing you at every stage of my career. He encouraged me to trust him and not walk in fear. In that moment of uncertainty, God reminded me of who he was. Apart of handling success is also leaning on your faith.

Two overarching questions to help you gauge where you are on this journey, what's your heart posture? and what's your level of character? You might wonder how these are connected. Ask yourself: if you achieve the success you desire, will you still advocate for others? How will you treat the people around you? What's your "why"? Will you achieve success and forget about the source that helped you get there? Will you get caught up in workplace drama and politics? These are important considerations that can help you assess your heart posture and level of character as you pursue success.

When you are on God's success plan, there is nothing that people can do to hurt you the way they think it can. You will outlast the naysayers, those who speak harm on your name, those who lie, those who judge you, etc. Your success is not co-dependent upon your work. Your success depends on you living out your purpose and assignment, which must come to pass because it's God's will.

We should all approach success like Cuban fishermen. This past February I spent about six hours in Cuba relaxing and watching local fishermen in Old

Havana. According to a recent report, 72% of Cubans live below the poverty line. So it's fair to suggest that these fishermen were either fishing for food they could take directly to their table or selling at a local market. As I watched them I couldn't imagine the pressure they must have been under to provide for their families. While most of us may have not have been so calm under those circumstances, especially due to the culture and how conditioned we are to be so fast paced in the USA. The more I hung out with them the more I noticed something unique about their posture. Amid the pressure of their circumstances they were calm, focused, patient, unmoved, quiet, and even helped each other. The character and attributes they displayed changed my perspective on the journey and process of maintaining any level of success. I wonder how our lives would be different if we embodied some of these characteristics of the Cuban fisherman. We should learn to stop putting our success on these strict timelines or against others. I too am guilty of this at times, I've come to learn whether I wanted to or not that God's timing is EVERYTHING, and its specially set-aside to ensure your success.

In the kingdom, when you impact one person, our success matters just the same as impacting 10K. Somewhere in our lives we were conditioned to believe that our success should solely be based on metrics, the education you've obtained, dollar signs, and likes on social media. I believe that this has done more harm to us than good. Our mental health is also negatively impacted when we fall into the "trap of comparison". Changing your belief system about success is the first step to actually obtaining success.

We limit our capacity for success by thinking that we lack the right relationships due to our environment. Some relationships that you will need for success only are meant for "seasons" and when we have developed unhealthy attachments and a "fear" of losing relationships, it limits God's ability to maximize our success to different levels if that's his ultimate desire. I believe that we only need a willingness to take the first step and God will always do the rest. He will send the right people along the journey to help teach us lessons, provide insight, and encourage us towards our purpose.

One of the early key relationships in my life that helped change my trajectory was with my Sociology Professor, Dr. James Butler from Nicholls State University in Thibodaux, LA. A few months after I got arrested for fighting on campus, he stopped me in the hallway and asked me why I was always late to his class. He was also quick to remind me that he had no issue "failing" me if I didn't put more focus in my studies. I visited his office almost every few months to talk about my academic, career, and life goals. The more I told him about my life, the more he was transparent about the challenges he thought I would face and work that I needed to do if I desired to be successful after in personal and professional life. He never judged me but always ended out conversations with encouragement, always sure to remind me that he believed in me and that despite my life's circumstances, whether I could see it or not, I was going to do great things.

Dr. Butler was one of the first positive male role models I had the opportunity to encounter as I grew into young adulthood. He spoke over me in a way that only a father-figure could. He held me accountable for my own success and journey. Through his mentorship, I learned the power of relationships and purpose. God loves us so much that he will send us the right people at the right time to help shift our trajectory towards success. He already knows our environmental challenges and limitations, and he also knows what he's already put in us to be successful along with our purpose. No matter where you are in life right now or what you think you don't have, pray for the right relationships to help you grow and evolve into your highest self. You may also be thinking that maybe you did encounter some of these trajectory shifting relationships and you decided not to engage, reject, or wasn't fully aware of the person's position in your life. Give yourself grace and take a moment to reflect to consider how many of these types of relationships you have not embraced that could be impacting your journey to success. Also take some time to reflect on how you plan to ensure that you are better able to identify and cultivate relationships with these individuals in the future. The key here is to understand your purpose to ensure that you are able to identify the right type of relationships that are God sent to help you maximize your sphere of influence.

One and one of the keys to life that I have learned is that everything you desire and want becomes available to you once you commit to your purpose but you must remember that success is not about you! For instance, my entire book and platform are focused on inspiring millennials to live a purposeful life. Purpose saved my life and it was the only thing that gave me meaning when nothing else did. Purpose has been the place where I have been able to grow and understand more about myself and the world around me. Living a purposeful life means understanding that you are here to have a human experience. Your primary focus should be to do what you were created to do, which will put you in spaces where you can communicate a message that helps change the world. Understanding your core purpose and function on earth is crucial. If you understand that success is not about you and live your life with humility, you will not only have a healthier view of success, but you will also be able to handle the success that comes your way.

Our work is about helping others grow, and should embrace that we all have unique ways of living that out. We are all equal, with different jobs, careers, passions, and so on, but our focus should be on how much we can impact others through our purpose. When we remove ourselves from the equation and focus on our core purpose, we can serve in any capacity and see it as just one aspect of our overall being or service.

Your purpose may be to advocate for youth in the juvenile justice system. However, you may live out that assignment in various capacities. You may function as a lawyer or judge, lead your own non-profit or mentoring organization, or be the CEO of a company that provides books to juveniles. One central purpose but different functions. Our thinking must shift to the idea that as we grow, if God sees fit to transition us into a different function to serve the same purpose, we are able to make such adjustments. Our assignment is never about "us" to begin with. The work is about those that we are here to SERVE.

Whether we become a big-time CEO or an assistant and eventually make that climb, we won't become arrogant and stay centered on our core.

Everyone's definition and levels of success, which they believe should be the "standard," will always be totally different. Too many internal and external contributing factors shape what success may look like in someone's life. If you are someone who perhaps came from less fortune experiences and you had to always live with "lack", you may work to ensure that you have the "basics" of life consistently in place and at times enjoy some things that you like. This is success to you and that's all that matters! Take it one step at a time. I am not saying don't evolve but who cares if you don't pursue the big degrees, jobs, at the same rate as others or even at all etc. No one knows your background but you, and you must always seek God's will for your life. Plant where you find fulfillment and allow God to take care of the rest. God knows what's best for you and will always give you the measure of success that you can handle at that time. It's about purpose not status! God will position and grow you in the way that he desires. I have found that as we attempt to run on this hamster wheel of trying to be what culture and other societal norms have defined as successful, we fall into the trap of comparison. We then begin a continuous evaluation cycle because we think something must be wrong with us if we have not experienced a certain level of success by a certain period or in the story we have told ourselves. We sometimes make our journey about this chase so much that we don't enjoy those critical moments and milestones along the way. I have seen all too often how when the pursuit of success is higher than one's core and central purpose, individuals intentionally or unintentionally find themselves doing whatever is necessary to obtain it, even if that means hurting people and comprising their morals along the way. The reality is that the same effort required to obtain said success will be the same effort required to maintain it. We chase success so much and make the pursuit of it so "loud" that we don't turned down the volume to help us enjoy those critical moments and milestones along the way. If we truly practice this, I think that we will understand that we are all a "success".

Many millennials get disappointed when their ideas of success don't pan out how they desired. As I have stated earlier in this chapter, God doesn't view success in the same way we do. For example, if you are passionate about helping the elderly and decide to create a non-profit organization to provide resources to nursing homes. While it's important to set organizational development and fundraising goals, you sometimes get discouraged if you don't achieve our desired level of success and even question our commitment to the cause. This is a normal human response to anything we set our minds to, but we must change our beliefs about success. In the nursing home example, you then provide resources for one nursing home and 100 residents. Even if your goal was to help five facilities, we must check-in with ourselves and remember the 100 families we are impacting. This is still a significant accomplishment and a form of success that you should celebrate as an accomplishment, even if just a milestone in your long term plan. This mindset shift takes hard and intentional work but worth the effort.

If you're like me, you may sometimes find it hard to celebrate your success. Sometimes it's because of the day-to-day grind, and we are not as fully present as we'd like. Or it's because of some deeper underlying issue, such as battling with "false humility." Regardless of where you stand in this area of your life, I want you to commit to celebrating your success. No matter how big or small, carve out some time to celebrate yourself. Take time to speak positive words about what you have accomplished every milestone you have achieved in your life. When you commit to celebrating yourself louder than anyone else could, you won't spend your life looking for others to celebrate you. Your growth and accomplishments won't depend on whether or not someone celebrates you. Whether they do or not, that human desire for affirmation will have been fulfilled by yourself. Imagine spending the rest of your life working so hard to achieve a milestone, and when you see people celebrate you, you move forward. But when they don't, you become stagnant. Why allow people to keep you on an emotional seesaw? Making this type of life change will help you take away the power of being controlled by someone else's affirmation or celebration of your life. It will also give you a sense of freedom and connectedness at your core. Repeat this daily affirmation,

> "I am committed to turning down the volume of success in my life. I will do the work to celebrate success as it comes to me, not compare, and remain humble if God CHOOSES to advance me to higher levels. But if he doesn't than I will be content because I am already a success".

Chapter 8
Closing

The choice of title for this project, *'Turn Down the Volume,'* was intentional, and chosen to inspire you that in order to grow and evolve into your purpose, you must practice turning down the volume of insecurities, people, and your view of success. As humans, we will always have to fight these inner battles of insecurities, people, and beliefs about success in our minds. We must also be committed to doing the necessary work to turn down the volume so that these inner battles are not louder than the voice that encourages, motivates, and gives direction, helping us live out the purpose of our lives.

My life's legacy will be and for many of you as well that it doesn't matter what background you come from - you matter! You were created with a purpose, and this book was designed to be a tool to help you get there. It's easy to try to be someone else or who everyone else wants you to be. But remember that aren't supposed to fit in - you are supposed to be different. You were supposed to stand out from the crowd. There is nothing about you that's accidental. You have talents, gifts, and a unique personality needed to change the world. You have a message to share that will impact the trajectory of your life and the lives of those connected to you. I hope this "Turning Down the Volume" project challenges you to continue evolving and I pray we all continue to heal, let go of perfectionism, and turn down the volume of **INSECURITIES, PEOPLE, & BELIEFS ABOUT SUCCESS** as you live life **ON PURPOSE!**

www.ingramcontent.com/pod-product-compliance
Lightning Source LLC
Chambersburg PA
CBHW050440010526
44118CB00013B/1610